A
CHRISTMAS
GARLAND

A CHRISTMAS GARLAND

CELIA HADDON

Michael Joseph
LONDON

To Lucy Parsons

MICHAEL JOSEPH LTD

Published by the Penguin Group
27 Wrights Lane, London W8 5TZ
Viking Penguin Inc., 375 Hudson Street, New York,
New York 10014, USA
Penguin Books Australia Ltd, Ringwood, Victoria, Australia
Penguin Books Canada Ltd, 10 Alcorn Avenue,
Toronto, Ontario, Canada M4V 3B2
Penguin Books (NZ) Ltd, 182-190 Wairau Road,
Auckland 10, New Zealand

Penguin Books Ltd, Registered Offices:
Harmondsworth, Middlesex, England

First published in Great Britain in 1995
This anthology copyright © by Celia Haddon 1995

Typeset in Baskerville 9½/10 point
Reprographics by Goodfellow & Egan, England
Printed in Singapore by Kyodo
Design and computer page make-up by Penny Mills

A CIP catalogue record for this book is available from
the British Library

ISBN 0 7181 3896 1

The moral right of the author has been asserted

CONTENTS

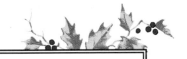

WELCOME CHRISTMAS

Now thrice welcome, Christmas,
Which brings us good cheer,
Minced pies and plum porridge,
Good ale and strong beer;
With pig, goose and capon,
The best that may be,
So well doth the weather
And our stomachs agree.

With holly and ivy,
So green and so gay,
We deck up our houses
As fresh as the day;
With bay and rosemary
And laurel complete;
And everyone now
Is a king in conceit.

ANONYMOUS,
seventeenth century

CHRISTMAS SHALL BE MERRY

Christmas time! That man must be a misanthrope indeed, in whose breast something like jovial feeling is not roused – in whose mind some pleasant associations are not awakened – by the recurrence of Christmas. There are people who will tell you that Christmas is not to them what it used to be: that each succeeding Christmas has found some cherished hope, or happy prospect, of the year before, dimmed or passed away, and that the present only serves to remind them of reduced circumstances and straitened incomes – of the feasts they once bestowed on hollow friends, and of the cold looks that meet them now, in adversity and misfortune. Never heed such dismal reminiscences. There are few men who have lived long enough in the world, who cannot call up such thoughts any day in the year. Then do not select the merriest of the three hundred and sixty five, for your doleful recollections, but draw your chair nearer the blazing fire – fill the glass and send round the song – and if your room be smaller than it was a dozen years ago, or if your glass be filled with reeking punch, instead of sparkling wine, put a good face on the matter, and empty it off hand, and fill another, and troll off the old ditty you used to sing, and thank God it's no worse. Reflect upon your present blessings – of which every man has many – not on your past misfortunes, of which all men have some. Fill your glass again, with a merry face and contented heart. Our life upon it, but your Christmas shall be merry, and your New Year a happy one.

CHARLES DICKENS

A CHRISTMAS PUDDING

Two pounds of suet-beef, quite fresh, and you must chop it fine;
One pound of raisins you must stone (on stones you could not dine);
One pound of bright sultanas pick, and in the bowl you'll mix
One pound of currants clean and dry, all free from grit or sticks.
A quarter pound of peel comes next, the *mixed* peel is not dear -
Orange and lemon, citron chips, this season's, fresh and clear;
Three ounces next of
   almonds chop, the bitter
   ones please use;
One pound of sugar you
   require, the Demerara
   choose.

One and half pounds of flour come
   next, let it be dry and sound;
One pound of bread crumbs follows
   suit; be sure they're finely
   ground.
Nine eggs next take and whisk them well,
   one nutmeg, only, add;
(To make things 'nice' with too
   much spice, in every way is bad).
Then take of salt a teaspoonful,
   stirred in with careful hand,
A pint of milk instead of beer, and
   you've a pudding grand!

ANONYMOUS

[10]

UPON THY PATH MAY HEAVENLY SUNBEAMS PLAY,
AND BRING TO THEE A MERRY CHRISTMAS DAY.

FROM THE NEW YORK *SUN*,
21 September, 1897

Dear Editor:

I am eight years old.
Some of my little friends say there is no Santa
Claus. Papa says, 'If you see it in *The Sun* it's so.'
Please tell me the truth, is there a Santa Claus?

Virginia O'Hanlon,   115 West 95th Street,

New York

Virginia, your little friends are wrong. They have been affected by the scepticism of a sceptical age. They do not believe except they see. They think that nothing can be, which is not comprehensible by their little minds. All minds, Virginia, whether they be men's or children's, are little. In this great universe of ours man is a mere insect, an ant, in his intellect, as compared with the boundless world about him, as measured by the intelligence capable of grasping the whole of truth and knowledge.

Yes, Virginia, there is a Santa Claus. He exists as certainly as love and generosity and devotion exist, and you know that they abound and give to your life its highest beauty and joy. Alas! how dreary would be the world if there were no Santa Claus! It would be as dreary as if there were no Virginias. There would be no childlike faith then, no poetry, no romance to make tolerable this existence. We should have no enjoyment, except in sense and sight. The eternal light with which childhood fills the world would be extinguished.

Not believe in Santa Claus! You might as well not believe in fairies! You might get your papa to hire men to watch in all the chimneys on Christmas Eve to catch Santa Claus, but even if they did not see Santa Claus coming down, what would that prove? Nobody sees Santa Claus, but that is no sign there is no Santa Claus. The most real things in the world are those that neither children nor men can see. Did you ever see fairies dancing on the lawn? Of course not, but that's no proof that they are not there. Nobody can conceive or imagine all the wonders there are unseen and unseeable in the world.

You tear apart the baby's rattle and see what makes the noise inside, but there is a veil covering the unseen world which not the strongest man, nor even the united strength of all the strongest men that ever lived, could tear apart. Only faith, fancy, poetry, love, romance, can push aside that curtain and view and picture the supernal beauty and glory beyond. Is it all real? Ah, Virginia, in all this world there is nothing else real and abiding. No Santa Claus! Thank God he lives, and he lives for ever. A thousand years from now, Virginia, nay ten times ten thousand years from now, he will continue to make glad the heart of childhood.

A MERRY CHRISTMAS TO YOU.

WINTER

In rigorous hours, when down the iron lane
The redbreast looks in vain
For hips and haws,
Lo, shining flowers upon my window-pane
The silver pencil of the winter draws.

When all the snowy hill
And the bare woods are still;
When snipes are silent in the frozen bogs,
And all the garden garth is whelmed in mire,
Lo, by the hearth, the laughter of the logs –
More fair than roses, lo, the flowers of fire!

ROBERT LOUIS STEVENSON

FALLOW DEER AT
THE LONELY HOUSE

One without looks in tonight
    Through the curtain-chink
From the sheet of glistening white;
One without looks in tonight
    As we sit and think
    By the fender-brink.

We do not discern those eyes
    Watching in the snow;
Lit by lamps of rosy dyes
We do not discern those eyes
    Wondering, aglow,
    Fourfooted, tiptoe.

THOMAS HARDY

THE OWL SONG

When icicles hang by the wall,
And Dick the shepherd blows his nail;
And Tom bears logs into the hall,
And milk comes frozen home in pail:
When blood is nipped, and ways be foul,
Then nightly sings the staring owl,
To-whit, to-who – a merry note,
While greasy Joan doth keel the pot.

When all aloud the wind doth blow,
And coughing drowns the parson's saw;
And birds sit brooding in the snow,
And Marian's nose looks red and raw:
When roasted crabs hiss in the bowl,
Then nightly sings the staring owl,
To-whit, to-who – a merry note,
While greasy Joan doth keel the pot.

WILLIAM SHAKESPEARE

HEART CALLETH TO HEART

Of all the old festivals, however, that of Christmas awakens the strongest and most heart-felt associations. It is a beautiful arrangement that this festival, which commemorates the announcement of the religion of peace and love, has been made the season for gathering together of family connections, and drawing closer again those bands of kindred hearts, which the cares and pleasures and sorrows of the world are continually operating to cast loose: of the calling back the children of a family, who have launched forth in life, and wandered widely asunder, once more to assemble about the paternal hearth, that rallying place of the affections, there to grow young and loving again among the endearing mementoes of childhood.

There is something in the very season of the year that gives a charm to the festivity of Christmas. In the depth of winter, when nature lies despoiled of every charm, and wrapped in her shroud of sheeted snow, we turn for our gratifications to moral sources. The dreariness and desolation of the landscape, the short gloomy days and darksome nights, while they circumscribe our wanderings, shut in our feelings also from rambling abroad, and make us more keenly disposed for the pleasure of the social circle. Our thoughts are more concentrated: our friendly sympathies more aroused. We feel more sensibly the charm of each other's society, and are brought more closely together by dependence on each other for enjoyment. Heart calleth unto heart; and we draw our pleasures from the deep wells of loving-kindness, which lie in the quiet recesses of our bosoms.

WASHINGTON IRVING

TO A SNOW-FLAKE

What heart could have thought you? –
Past our devisal
(O filigree petal!)
Fashioned so purely,
Fragilely, surely,
From what Paradisal
Imagineless metal,
Too costly for cost?
Who hammered you, wrought you,
From argentine vapour? –
'God was my shaper.
Passing surmisal,
He hammered, He wrought me,
From curled silver vapour,
To lust of His mind: –
So purely, so palely,
Tinily, surely,
Mightily, frailly,
Insculped and embossed,
With His hammer of wind,
And His graver of frost.'

Francis Thompson

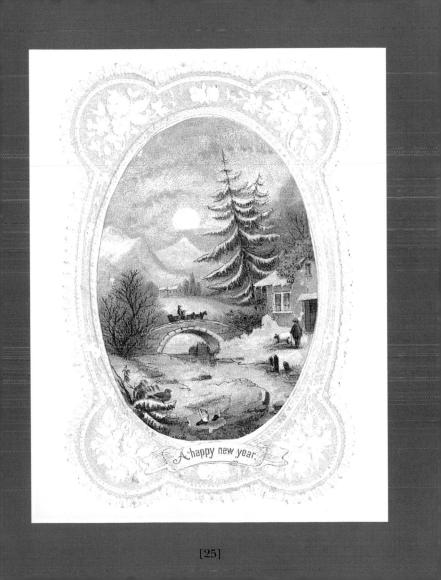

A happy new year.

CHRISTMAS CAROLS

It is in the old Christmas carols, the carols which date from the Middle Ages, that we find not only what makes Christmas poetic and soothing and stately, but first and foremost what makes Christmas exciting. The exciting quality of Christmas rests on an ancient and admitted paradox. It rests upon the great paradox that the power and centre of the whole universe may be found in some seemingly small matter, that the stars in their courses may move like a moving wheel round the neglected outhouse of an inn. When Walt Whitman said, 'There is no object so soft but it makes a hub for the wheeled universe,' he expressed unconsciously what is the thrilling element in the story of Bethlehem. And it is extraordinary to

notice how completely this feeling of the paradox of the manger was lost by the brilliant and ingenious theologians, and how com`-pletely it was kept in the Christmas carols. They, at least, never forgot that the main business of the story they had to tell was that the absolute once ruled the universe from a cattle stall.

There is a small and vulgar fashion of discouraging carols at Christmas. People who chat cheerfully amid all the infernal noises of the underground, people who endure the rattle of a thousand vehicles over a stony road, pretend that they dislike the sound of Christmas carols. To pretend to like a thing may be a sin: to pretend to dislike a thing comes near to the sin against the Holy Ghost. At least it may be hoped that a few at this season may listen to these songs: they are the last echoes of the cry that renewed the world.

G.K. CHESTERTON

GOD'S MOTHER

I sing of a maiden
That is makeless;
King of all kings
To her son she ches.

He came all so still
Where his mother was
As dew in April
That falleth on the grass.

He came all so still
Where his mother lay
As dew in April
That falleth on the spray.

He came all so still
To his mother's bower
As dew in April
That falleth on the flower.

Mother and maiden
Was never none but she;
Well may such a lady
Godès mother be.

ANONYMOUS,
fifteenth century

Peace on earth Goodwill toward men

A Happy

Christmas

HERE IS NOTHING I CAN GIVE YOU …

There is nothing I can give you, which you have not,
But there is much, very much that while I cannot give it,
   you can take.

No heaven can come to us unless our hearts find rest in today. Take
   heaven!

No peace lies in the future, which is not hidden in this present
   instant. Take peace!

The gloom of the world is but a shadow.

Behind it, yet within reach, is joy.

There is a radiance and glory in the darkness, could we but see,

And to see we have only to look. I beseech you to look.

Life is so generous a giver, but we, judging its gifts by their covering,
   cast them away as ugly, or heavy or hard.

Remove the covering, and you will find beneath it a living
   splendour, woven of love, by wisdom with power.

Welcome it, grasp it, and you touch the angel's hand that brings it
   to you.

Everything we call a trial, a sorrow, or a duty, believe me that the
   angel's hand is there; the gift is there and the wonder of an
   overshadowing presence.

Our joys too: be not content with them as joys.

They, too, conceal diviner gifts.

And so, at this time I greet you.

Not quite as the world sends greetings, but with profound esteem
   and with the prayer that for you now and forever, the day breaks,
   and the shadows flee away.

ATTRIBUTED TO FRA GIOVANNI, 1513

CHRISTMAS FARE

Good husband and huswife, now chiefly be glad
Things handsome to have, as they ought to be had;
They both do provide, against Christmas do come,
To welcome their neighbours, good cheer to have some.

Good bread and good drink, a good fire in the hall,
Brawn, pudding and souse, and good mustard withal.
Beef, mutton, and pork, and good pies of the best,
Pig, veal, goose, and capon, and turkey well dressed:
Cheese, apples, and nuts, and good carols to hear,
As then in the country is counted good cheer.

What cost to good husband is any of this?
Good household provision only it is;
Of other the like I do leave out a many,
That costeth the husband never a penny.

THOMAS TUSSER

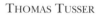

ST FRANCIS OF ASSISI AND THE ANIMALS AT CHRISTMAS

Those of us who were with St. Francis and wrote these things down, bear witness to the fact that we heard him say many times: 'If I were to speak with the Emperor, I would beg and persuade him by the love of God and of myself, to create a special decree that nobody capture or kill our sisters the larks nor do them any harm. Likewise that all the rulers of towns and villages, and commanders of fortresses, be bound to compel their kinsmen on Christmas day every year to throw corn and other grains on to the roads outside the towns and fortresses, so that our sisters the larks and indeed other birds, might have something to eat on such a holy day. Also that, out of reverence for the Son of God, for Whom on that night the Blessed Virgin Mary lay down between an ox and an ass in a stable, whoever owns an ox or an ass be made to feed them especially well on that night, and similarly on that night the poor have their fill of good food from the rich.'

BROTHER LEO

The Compliments

THE BALLAD OF THE STORK

The stork she rose on Christmas Eve,
And said unto her brood,
'I now must fare to Bethlehem
To view the Son of God.'

She gave to each his dole of meat,
She stowed them fairly in:
And far she flew and fast she flew
And came to Bethlehem.

'Now where is He of David's line?'
She asked at house and hall.
'He is not here', they spake hardly,
'But in the manger stall.'

She found Him in the manger stall,
With that most holy Maid;
The gentle stork, she wept to see
The Lord so rudely laid.

Then from her panting breast she plucked
The feathers white and warm;
She strewed them in the manger bed
To keep the Lord from harm.

'Now blessèd be the gentle stork
For evermore,' quoth He,
'For that she saw my sad estate
And showèd such pity.

Full welcome shall she ever be
In hamlet and in hall,
And called henceforth the blessèd bird
And friend of babies all.'

TRADITIONAL
BALLAD

AN ANCESTOR OF OUR
CHRISTMAS TREE

My dear Sara,

At Christmas I saw a custom which pleased and interested me here. The children make little presents to their parents, and to one another, and the parents to the children. For three or four months before Christmas the girls are all busy, and the boys save up their pocket-money, to make or purchase these presents. What the present is to be is cautiously kept secret, and the girls have a world of contrivances to conceal it.

On the evening before Christmas Day, one of the parlours is lighted up by the children, into which the parents must not go. A great yew bough is fastened on the table at a little distance from the wall, a multitude of little tapers are fastened in the bough, but not so as to burn it, till they are nearly burnt out, and coloured paper, etc., hangs and flutters from the twigs. Under this bough the children lay out in great neatness the presents they mean for their parents, still concealing in their pockets what they intend for each other. Then the parents are introduced, and each presents his little gift – and then they bring out the others, and present them to each other with kisses and embraces.

SAMUEL TAYLOR COLERIDGE,
writing in 1799 from Northern Germany

THE NIGHT BEFORE
CHRISTMAS

'Twas the night before Christmas, when all through the house,
Not a creature was stirring, not even a mouse;
The stockings were hung by the chimney with care,
In the hope that St Nicholas soon would be there.
The children were nestled all snug in their beds,
While visions of sugar plums danced through their heads;
And mamma in her 'kerchief, and I in my cap,
Had just settled our brains for a long winter's nap,
When out on the lawn there arose such a clatter,
I sprang from my bed to see what was the matter.
The way to the window, I flew like a flash,
Tore open the shutters, and threw up the sash;
The moon on the breast of the new-fallen snow
Gave the lustre of midday to objects below.
When what to my wondering eyes should appear
But a miniature sleigh and eight tiny reindeer;
With a little old driver, so lively and quick,
I knew in a moment it must be St Nick.
More rapid than eagles his coursers they came,
And he whistled, and shouted, and called them by
    name –
'Now Dasher! now Dancer! Now Prancer! now
    Vixen!
On Comet! on Cupid! on Donder and Blixen!
To the top of the porch, to the top of the wall!
Now dash away! dash away! dash away all!'
As the leaves that before the wild hurricane fly,

When they meet with an obstacle, mount to the sky;
So up to the house-top the coursers they flew,
With the sleigh full of toys, and St Nicholas too.
And then in a twinkling I heard on the roof
The prancing and pawing of each little hoof;
As I drew in my head and was turning around,
Down the chimney St Nicholas came with a bound.
He was dressed all in furs from his head to his foot
And his clothes were all tarnished with ashes and soot.
A bundle of toys he had flung on his back,
And he looked like a pedlar just opening his pack.
His eyes how they twinkled! his dimples, how merry!
His cheeks were like roses, his nose like a cherry;
His droll little mouth was drawn up like a bow,
And the beard of his chin was as white as the snow.
The stump of a pipe he held tight in his teeth,
And the smoke it encircled his head like a wreath.
He had a broad face and a little round belly
That shook when he laughed, like a bowl full of jelly.
He was chubby and plump – a right jolly old elf;
And I laughed when I saw him, in spite of myself.
A wink of his eye and a twist of his head
Soon gave me to know I had nothing to dread.
He spoke not a word, but went straight to his work,
And filled all the stockings – then turned with a jerk,
And laying his finger aside of his nose,
And giving a nod, up the chimney he rose;
He sprang to his sleigh, to his team gave a whistle,
And away they all flew like the down of a thistle.
But I heard him exclaim, ere he drove out of sight,
'Happy Christmas to all, and to all a good night!'

CLEMENT CLARKE MOORE

[42]

THE OXEN

Christmas Eve, and twelve of the clock.
   'Now they are all on their knees,'
An elder said as we sat in a flock
   By the embers in hearthside ease.

We pictured the meek mild creatures where
   They dwelt in their strawy pen,
Nor did it occur to one of us there
   To doubt they were kneeling then.

So fair a fancy few would weave
   In these years! Yet, I feel,
If someone said on Christmas Eve,
   'Come; see the oxen kneel,

'In the lonely barton by yonder
   coomb
   Our childhood used to know,'
I should go with him in the gloom,
   Hoping it might be so.

                THOMAS HARDY

I SAW A STABLE

I saw a stable, low and very bare,
A little child in a manger.
The oxen knew Him, had Him in their care,
To men He was a stranger.
The safety of the world was lying there,
And the world's danger.

MARY COLERIDGE

THE NATIVITY

Where is this stupendous stranger,
Swains of Solyma, advise,
Lead me to my Master's manger,
Shew me where my Saviour lies?

Nature's decorations glisten
Far above their usual trim;
Birds on box and laurel listen,
As so near the cherubs hymn.

Boreas now no longer winters
On the desolated coast;
Oaks no more are riv'n in splinters
By the whirlwind and his host.

Spinks and ouzels sing sublimely,
'We too have a Saviour born';
Whiter blossoms burst untimely
On the blest Mosaic thorn.

God all-bounteous, all-creative,
Whom no ills from good dissuade,
Is incarnate, and a native
Of the very world he made.

CHRISTOPHER SMART

HOSPITALITY ON CHRISTMAS DAY

This day is worthily dedicated to be observed in remembrance of the blessed nativity of our Redeemer, Jesus Christ: at which time it pleased the Almighty Father to send his only begotten Son into the world for our sakes; and by an unspeakable union to join in one person God and man, without confusion of natures, or possibility of separation. To express, therefore, our thankfulness, and the joy we ought to have in this love of God, there hath been anciently, and is yet continued in England, a neighbourly and plentiful hospitality in inviting, and (without invitation) receiving unto our well-furnished tables, our tenants, neighbours, friends, and strangers: to the honour of our nation, and the increase of amity and free-hearted kindness among us. But, most of all, to the refreshing of the bowels of the poor, being the most Christian use of such festivals.

GEORGE WITHER

CHRISTMAS CUSTOMS

Old customs, O I love the sound
However simple they may be,
Whate'er with time has sanction found
Is welcome and is dear to me.
Pride grows above simplicity
And spurns it from her haughty mind,
And soon the poet's song will be
The only refuge they can find.

The shepherd now no more afraid
Since custom doth the chance bestow,
Starts up to kiss the giggling maid
Beneath the branch of mistletoe
That 'neath each cottage beam is seen
With pearl-like berries shining gay,
The shadow still of what hath been
Which fashion yearly fades away.

And oft for pence and spicy ale,
With winter nosegays pinned before,
The wassail singer tells her tale
And drawls her Christmas carols o'er.
The prentice boy with ruddy face
And rime-bepowdered dancing locks
From door to door with happy pace
Runs round to claim his 'Christmas box'.

JOHN CLARE

LEGEND OF
THE CHRISTMAS
ROSE

In the hellebores (*Helleborus niger*) we have Christmas Roses, not only lovely to the eye but appropriated to the season. Throughout northern Europe this plant is known as the Holy Night Rose, the Rose of Noel, or Christ's Flower or Bloom, and the origin of the names is worth the telling. In the old mystery plays of the Nativity, a maiden named Madelon was represented as coming with the shepherds to Bethlehem to see the great thing that had come to pass. She was very poor, and her woman's heart was so moved by the penury of the manger scene that she burst into tears at having nothing to offer to comfort the Blessed Mother and show her sympathy and love for the little Child. God, seeing her, sent Gabriel to her who said, 'Madelon, what makes you weep while you pray?' And she answered, 'My Lord, because I have nothing to offer the Infant Jesus; even if I had but some flowers to give him I should be happy, but it is winter, and the frost is in the ground and spring is far away'. Then the Herald of the Annunciation took her by the hand and led her forth into the dark night, but as they went the cold seemed gone. Gabriel paused and touched the rigid earth with his staff, and lo! on every side sprang up these pure blossoms of the Holy Night Rose, and running from his side the shepherd maiden filled her arms with their flowers to deck the cave upon the first Christmas Day.

ALFRED
DOWLING

We have seen his Star in the East

THE BURNING BABE

As I in hoary winter's night stood shivering in the snow,
Surprised I was with sudden heat which made my heart to glow;
And lifting up a fearful eye to view what fire was near,
A pretty Babe all burning bright did in the air appear;
Who scorchèd with excessive heat, such floods of tears did shed,
As though his floods should quench his flames which with his
    fears were fed.
'Alas!' quoth he, 'but newly born in fiery heats I fry,
Yet none approach to warm their hearts or feel my fire but I.
My faultless breast the furnace is, the fuel wounding thorns;
Love is the fire, and sighs the smoke, the ashes shame and
    scorns;
The fuel Justice layeth on, and Mercy blows the coals;
The metals in this furnace wrought are man's defilèd souls:
For which, as now on fire I am to work them to their good,
So will I melt into a bath to wash them in my blood.'
With this he vanished out of sight and swiftly shrunk away,
And straight I callèd unto mind that it was Christmas Day.

ROBERT SOUTHWELL

CELEBRATIONS

Not a cup of drink must pass without a carol, the beasts, fowl and fish come to a general execution, and the corn is ground to dust for the bakehouse, and the pastry: now good cheer and welcome, and God be with you, and I thank you, and against the new year, provide for the presents: the Lord of Mis-rule is no mean man for his time, and the guests of the high table must lack no wine: the lusty bloods must look about them like men, and piping and dancing puts away much melancholy: a good fire heats all the house, and a full alms-basket makes the beggars prayers: the maskers and the mummers make the merry sport: but if they lose their money, their drum goes dead: musicians now make their instruments speak out and a good song is worth the hearing. In sum, it is a holy time, a duty

in Christians, for the remembrance of Christ, and custom among friends, for the maintenance of good fellowship; in brief, I thus conclude of it. I hold it a memory of the Heaven's Love, and the world's peace, and the mirth of the honest and the meeting of the friendly.

NICHOLAS BRETON

TO GOD

Lord, I am like to mistletoe,
Which has no root, and cannot grow
Or prosper but by that same tree
It climbs about; so I by Thee.
What need I then to fear at all,
So long as I about Thee crawl?
But if that tree should fall and die,
Tumble shall heav'n, and down will I.

ROBERT HERRICK

A SMALL
MOMENT

Do I not share with most people a feeling of *aftermaths*, of slight psychic exhaustion, after a period of crowded pleasures and close neighbourliness? The enjoyment of them is intense, but then enjoyment is in itself a strenuous occupation, demanding every ounce of our energy, mental, physical and emotional. To entertain our families and friends we have to give all that we have within ourselves, or almost all. And afterwards, we are like the widow's cruse, temporarily empty. It is then that the ever-repeated miracle takes place, the unaccountable refuelling of the self within us. But we have to prepare for that miracle, and here again it is often not done deliberately, but by another act of external guidance, so that we wander away, in poverty of mood, to find ourselves seemingly but not actually by chance in the redeeming situation.

So I was led that night after Christmas. The last dinner party was over, the last car load gone. Before locking up, I went out into the lane with my two companions, the corgi and the white cat, to take a pace or two before creeping up to bed.

I felt the old year waning about me. That brings

always a solemn condition of mind. Time looms up ominously, looms and passes, a great train in darkness, roaring and vanishing, taking part of us with it, our other, younger selves, so many selves that they have become strangers to us, except for an identity of regrets …

In an English lane on a winter night, in the afterglow and depression following Christmas, there I stood with my cat and my dog, looking up at the night sky. Suddenly, with a wild break in formation, the swirling clouds opened, and there slid out from them the whole constellation of Orion, square and steady, with his belt glittering, his outriders like beacons, and following him, driving him on so briskly yet regally, his dog, the sun Sirius. There they hung, so clean-cut in the purple void, shining so fiercely that they seemed to dip and rise, dip and rise, by fractions of an inch, yet to ride steady, rushing westward through the vast silence. Then the clouds closed again, and the adventure was over. I had lived through an experience that might have taken a century to enact. I was enriched, humbled, my personal depression not dispersed but changed into something larger than myself, a quiet and utterly humble mood in which I resigned myself to the conquests by the years, the passing of all human achievements and possessions, and a recognition of the riches beyond them.

Then, half lost still, I felt a soft touch on my leg. The old cat, feeble with his age, was looking up at me, and the moonlight was spilled into his two great eyes. He murmured to me, and again lifted a padded foot to remind me where I was, and of my responsibility.

RICHARD CHURCH

AULD LANG SYNE

Should auld acquaintance be forgot,
And never brought to mind?
Should auld acquaintance be forgot,
And auld lang syne?

    For auld lang syne, my dear,
    For auld lang syne,
    We'll tak a cup o' kindness yet,
    For auld lang syne.

And surely ye'll be your pint stowp!
And surely I'll be mine;
And we'll tak a cup o' kindness yet
    For auld lang syne.

We twa have paidl'd in the burn,
From morning sun till dine;
But seas between us braid hae roar'd
    Sin' auld lang syne.

And there's a hand, my trusty fiere,
And gie's a hand o' thine;
And we'll tak a right gude-willie waught,
For auld lang syne.

ROBERT BURNS

Cheers for the Navy, and a Happy New Year!

RINGING OUT GLAD TIDINGS.

NEW YEAR BELLS

Ring out, wild bells, to the wild sky,
    The flying cloud, the frosty light:
    The year is dying in the night;
Ring out, wild bells, and let him die.

Ring out the old, ring in the new,
    Ring, happy bells, across the snow:
    The year is going, let him go;
Ring out the false, ring in the true.

Ring out the grief that saps the mind,
    For those that here we see no more;
    Ring out the feud of rich and poor,
Ring in redress to all mankind.

Ring out old shapes of foul disease;
    Ring out the narrowing lust of gold;
    Ring out the thousand wars of old,
Ring in the thousand years of peace.

Ring in the valiant man and free,
    The larger heart, the kindlier hand;
    Ring out the darkness of the land,
Ring in the Christ that is to be.

ALFRED, LORD TENNYSON

ACKNOWLEDGEMENTS

I have tried to obtain permission from all copyright holders, but there are some I could not trace. The publishers will be happy to rectify any omissions in future editions. I should like to thank the following for permission to reprint:

Robin McCoubrey, Peterhouse College, Cambridge, for his translation of Brother Leo's account of St Francis and the Animals at Christmas. The estate of Richard Church and Laurence Pollinger Ltd for an extract from 'Small Moments' by Richard Church. Macmillan, Ltd, London, for 'Fallow Deer at a Lonely House' and 'The Oxen' from *The Collected Poems of Thomas Hardy*. A.P. Watt on behalf of the Royal Literary Fund for a passage by G.K. Chesterton.